SCAM ARTISTS

»→ By Virginia Loh-Hagan ←«

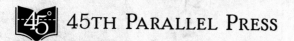

45TH PARALLEL PRESS

Published in the United States of America by Cherry Lake Publishing Group
Ann Arbor, Michigan
www.cherrylakepublishing.com

Reading Adviser: Beth Walker Gambro, MS, Ed., Reading Consultant, Yorkville, IL
Book Designer: Melinda Millward

Photo Credits: cover, title page: ©goffkein.pro/Shutterstock; page 7: © BestStockFoto/Shutterstock; page 9: © Dina Belenko/Shutterstock; page 11: © MongPro/Shutterstock; page 12: Frank Moss (1860-1920), Public domain, via Wikimedia Commons; page 15: © WildSnap/Shutterstock; page 17: © Andrey Julay/Shutterstock; page 19: © WDG Photo/Shutterstock; page 20: © Malochka Mikalai/Shutterstock; page 23: © kangwan nirach/Shutterstock; page 25: © YURY TARANIK/Shutterstock; page 27: © Jay Yuan/Shutterstock; page 29: © Africa Studio/Shutterstock

Graphic Element Credits: Cover, multiple interior pages: © marekuliasz/Shutterstock, © Andrey_Kuzmin/Shutterstock, © Here/Shutterstock

Library of Congress Cataloging-in-Publication Data has been filed and is available at catalog.loc.gov.

Cherry Lake Publishing Group would like to acknowledge the work of the Partnership for 21st Century Learning, a Network of Battelle for Kids. Please visit http://www.battelleforkids.org/networks/p21 for more information.

Printed in the United States of America
Corporate Graphics

About the Author

Dr. Virginia Loh-Hagan is an author and educator. She is currently the Director of the Asian Pacific Islander Desi American (APIDA) Center at San Diego State University and the Co-Executive Director of The Asian American Education Project. She lives in San Diego with her very tall husband and very naughty dogs. To learn more about her, follow her on Instagram @vlohhagan.

Note from publisher: Websites change regularly, and their future contents are outside of our control.
Supervise children when conducting any recommended online searches for extended learning opportunities.

TABLE OF CONTENTS

* * * * * * * * * * *
INTRODUCTION
* * * * * * * * * *

Imagine fooling people as a job. This is what **scam artists** do. **Scams** are tricks. Scam artists create fake plans. They pretend they're real. They lie. They cheat. They steal. They use other people. They do this to get money.

Scam artists are also con artists. "Con" stands for **confidence**. It means feeling trust. Scam artists put on an act. They gain people's trust. They win them over. Then they **defraud** them. Defraud means tricking people for money.

Some scam artists get caught. They miss details. They mix up lies. They ruin people's lives. Some get sent to jail. Some get away. Learn about famous scam artists in history.

CURRENT CASE:

Best-Dressed Scam Artist of the Year

✳ ✳ ✳ ✳ ✳ ✳ ✳ ✳ ✳ ✳

Anna Sorokin (born 1991) called herself Anna Delvey. She was born in Russia. She grew up in Germany. She moved to New York City in 2013. She said she was a rich German heiress. Sorokin said she had millions in Europe. She scammed wealthy people. She wanted to create an arts social club. Her club would be for private members. Sorokin created fake bank papers. She used fake checks. She tricked people into paying for her expenses. She wore designer clothes. She stayed in expensive hotels. She said she didn't want to be famous. She said, "I'd met people who were doing things. So, I was like why can't I do the same? I was trying to create my own opportunities." She wanted to make her own mark. She was sent to jail.

* * * * * * * * * * * *
MARY MODERS
(1642-1673)
* * * * * * * * * * * *

Mary Moders was from England. Her first husband was Thomas Stedman. Moders left him. But she did not get a divorce. She then married Thomas Day. Day was a doctor. Moders was jailed for **bigamy**. Bigamy is being married to more than one person at a time. Moders escaped. She went to Germany. A nobleman fell in love with her. She took his money and jewels.

Moders returned to England. She said she was a German princess. She scammed John Carleton. Carleton was a doctor. He married her. Moders is often known as Mary Carleton.

Someone sent John Carleton a letter. Moders was caught. She was sent to jail.

Moders became famous. She starred in a play about her life. She got many gifts. She married a fan. She scammed him. She did this for 10 years. She was later caught. She was put to death.

Mary Moders was arrested for stealing a silver mug. She was sent to Jamaica. She escaped. She went back to England. She was sentenced to death.

WILLIAM ROCKEFELLER SR.

(1810–1906)

* * * * * * * * * * * *

William Rockefeller Sr. was born in New York. He was known as "Devil Bill." He was a traveling salesman. He called himself Dr. William Levingston. He made and sold potions. He sold snake oil. He said this oil cured everything.

Rockefeller faked not being able to hear. He faked not being able to speak. People felt sorry for him. They bought things from him.

Rockefeller bought land. He gave loans to farmers. Some couldn't pay him back. So he took their land. He made a lot of money.

Rockefeller was a bigamist. As Dr. Levingston, he married Margaret Allen (1834–1910). As a Rockefeller, he married Eliza Davison (1813–1889). His son with Eliza was John D. Rockefeller (1839–1937). John was the world's first billionaire. He avoided connections to his father.

William Rockefeller Sr. sold snake oil as Dr. William Levingston. He told people it cured everything.

GEORGE WASHINGTON APPO
(1856–1930)

Pickpockets steal from people's pockets. George Washington Appo was one of the best. He picked thousands of pockets. He led a life of crime. At a young age, he sold newspapers. He got close to people. He stole from their pockets. He was also part of a **green goods scam**. He tricked people into buying fake money.

Appo was in and out of jail. He went to court many times. He became famous. His manner of speech was copied by many. He was the model for criminals in movies. He's known for saying things like "youse guys." He's known for making a slicing motion with his hand.

George Washington Appo wrote a book about himself.
He also starred in a play about his life.

George Washington Appo (center) changed pickpocketing. The new style of pickpocketing that Appo used is on the left. The old style of pickpocketing is on the right.

Appo came from a criminal family. He was born in Connecticut. His mother was Irish American. His father was Chinese American. His father had killed someone. He was the first Asian American to be **convicted** in New York. Convicted means to be found guilty. Appo's mother died soon after. Appo scammed to survive.

COLD CASE:

The Unsolved Mystery of the D.B. Cooper Hijacking

No one knows who D.B. Cooper is. Even his name is fake. On November 24, 1971, he went to the airport in Portland, Oregon. He wore a dark suit. He wore dark sunglasses. He had a black bag. He bought a plane ticket. He got on Flight 305. The plane left Portland. It was heading to Seattle. Cooper sat in the back. He gave a note to the flight attendant. He said, "Miss, you'd better look at that note. I have a bomb." He asked for $200,000 in cash. He asked for parachutes. He got everything he wanted. He told the pilot to fly to Mexico City. Then he jumped. He used his parachute. It's the only unsolved plane hijacking. Hijack means to take over a plane. The FBI searched for years. They stopped in 2016. They only found some of the money. Many think Cooper died during the fall. He was never found.

* * * * * * * * * * * *
ELIZABETH BIGLEY
(1857–1907)
* * * * * * * * * * * * *

Andrew Carnegie (1835–1919) was one of the richest Americans. Cassie L. Chadwick claimed to be his daughter. She said her mother was Carnegie's lover. She said Carnegie gave her money. She said she'd inherit his money. People believed her. Banks believed her. They loaned her millions. She never paid them back.

Chadwick was lying. Her real name was Elizabeth Bigley. She was from Canada. She started scamming at a young age. She changed her name several times. She wrote fake letters of inheritance. She claimed to be an **heiress**. An heiress inherits family money. Bigley did this often.

She went to jail several times. Carnegie went to one of her trials. He said, "I have not signed a note in the last 30 years." He said no one asked him.

Elizabeth Bigley was called the "Queen of Ohio." She bought diamonds. She bought clothes.

WILLIAM THOMPSON

(1800s)

Not much is known about William Thompson. In 1849, a newspaper wrote about him. It called him a "confidence man." This started the term "con man."

Thompson scammed rich people in New York City. He did this in the late 1840s. He dressed nicely. He would go up to a rich person. He acted like they knew each other. He'd start talking. He'd gain their trust. Then he'd ask, "Have you confidence in me to trust me with your watch until tomorrow?" People didn't want to offend him. They gave him their watches. Thompson took the watches. He'd leave. He'd never return the watches.

In 1849, he was caught. One of his victims saw him walking in the street. He reported Thompson. The police found him. Thompson was jailed.

Thompson stole many expensive watches with his con.

VICTOR LUSTIG
(1890-1947)

Victor Lustig spoke 5 languages. He had more than 20 fake names. He scammed many people.

The Eiffel Tower is in Paris, France. It's famous. Lustig tried to sell it. He said he was a government official. He said France was tearing down the tower. He said his job was to sell the metal. He said it was a secret deal. Scrap dealers believed him. One dealer gave Lustig money. Lustig took it. He fled town.

Six months later, Lustig returned. He did the same scam. This time, he was caught. Newspapers wrote

The Eiffel Tower was built as an entrance to the
1889 World's Fair. It wasn't meant to be permanent.
Victor Lustig shared this with his victims.

Al Capone gave Victor Lustig money as a reward when he thought Lustig was being honest.

about it. Lustig fled to the United States.

He kept scamming. He tried to sell a special box. He said the box made fake money. He even scammed Al Capone (1899–1947). Capone was a crime boss. He gave Lustig money for a scam. Lustig kept the money. But then he returned it. He said the scam didn't work. Capone thought Lustig was honest. He gave him a reward. That's what Lustig wanted.

WORST-CASE SCENARIO:

How a Scam Got Its Name

* * * * * * * * * *

Would you like a scam to be named after you? A Ponzi scheme is fraud. It's a fake business. Scam artists say they have a great deal. People give them money. They expect to earn more money. But the deal is fake. There are no profits. People are paid with money from others. Scam artists take the money. Ponzi schemes have robbed billions from people. They're still happening. They're named after Charles Ponzi (1882–1949). Ponzi sold international postage stamps. He bought them from one country. He traded them in another. He tricked people. He said this was a big business. He made a lot of money. His scam was big. It was popular. But he was not the first. Sarah Howe (c. 1826–1892) did it before him. But the scheme isn't named after her. Howe is from Boston. She created a fake bank. She only took money from single women.

* * * * * * * * * * * * *
SUSANNA MILDRED HILL
(c. 1880s–1940s)
* * * * * * * * * * * * *

Much of Susanna Mildred Hill's life is unknown. But what is known is that she broke many hearts. She fooled many men. In the 1940s, she wrote love letters. She had many male **pen pals**. Pen pals write letters to each other.

Hill was in her 60s. But she told her pen pals she was in her 20s. She said she was a pretty young woman. Men believed her. They fell in love with her. They sent her money. They sent her gifts. They never met her.

This trick is called the "Lonely Hearts Scam." It still happens. Today, it's called **catfishing**. Scammers steal pictures of attractive people. They post them online. They lure victims that way.

Today, people email and text. They don't often write letters.

* * * * * * * * * * * *
MITHILESH KUMAR SRIVASTAVA
(1912–2009)
* * * * * * * * * * *

Mithilesh Kumar Srivastava was known as Natwarlal. He was India's most famous scam artist. He stole from the rich. He gave money to his poor village. This made him a hero.

Natwarlal was a master **forger**. Forge means to copy. His forging started at a young age. A neighbor sent him to the bank. Natwarlal forged his neighbor's signature. He took his neighbor's money. He fled to the city of Calcutta.

Natwarlal studied banking. He forged many papers.

He committed more than 100 crimes. He was sentenced to 113 years in jail. But he scammed his way out. He escaped jail 8 times. Once, he wore a police uniform. He gave guards what he said was a suitcase of money. The suitcase held newspapers instead.

He even scammed his death. His lawyer said he died in 2009. But his brother said he died in 1996.

Natwarlal tried to sell many famous Indian buildings. For example, he tried to sell the Taj Mahal. This building is a king's tomb.

✳ ✳ ✳ ✳ ✳ ✳ ✳ ✳ ✳ ✳ ✳
DAVID HAMPTON
(1964-2003)
✳ ✳ ✳ ✳ ✳ ✳ ✳ ✳ ✳ ✳ ✳

Sidney Poitier (1927-2022) was an actor. He was the first Black man to win an Academy Award for Best Actor. He was famous. He was handsome.

David Hampton was born in Buffalo, New York. He moved to New York City in the 1980s. He tried to get into a popular night club. The club would not admit him. Hampton said he was Poitier's son. His trick worked. He was treated like a star.

Hampton kept up the scam. He called himself David Poitier. He told rich people he was Poitier's son. He said he'd missed his plane. Or he told them he had been robbed. People believed him. They gave him money. They gave him food. They gave him places to stay.

Hampton was caught. People based a play on his story. They made a movie, too. The play and movie are called *Six Degrees of Separation*.

David Hampton also claimed he went to Harvard University.

✳✳✳✳✳✳✳✳✳✳✳✳
SYLVIA BROWNE
(1936-2013)
✳ ✳ ✳ ✳ ✳ ✳ ✳ ✳ ✳ ✳ ✳ ✳

Sylvia Browne was from Missouri. She said she had special powers. She saw **visions** starting at age 3. Visions are like dreams with meaning. Browne said she was a **medium**. Mediums claim they can talk to spirits. Browne said she could talk to the dead. She said she could see the past. She said she could see the future.

Browne gave **readings**. Readings are like fortune telling. People paid her. She did well. She answered questions over the phone. She started her own companies.

Browne said she could help the police. She said she could find missing people. But her comments were wrong. Many thought she was a fraud.

Sylvia Browne did readings. Palm reading is a type of reading.

FOR YOUR EYES ONLY...

* * * * * * * * * * *

HOW TO BE A SCAM ARTIST!*

Do you want to be a scam artist? Do you have what it takes? Here are 3 tips:

Tip #1: Know your mark.

Create trust with marks. Marks are victims. They're marked as targets. Connect with them. Learn all about them. Get a **shill**. Shills are partners in crime. They tell marks you're real.

Tip #2: Look real.

Spend money to make money. Give a small payout. This shows the deal is real. Gain trust. Build a good story.

Tip #3: Scam and scram.

Force marks to act quickly. Leave as soon as you can. Say time is running out. Say other people want in. Don't give people time to think.

*WARNING: Scam artists can go to jail. They can make people angry. Don't be a scam artist.

ICYW: IN CASE YOU'RE WONDERING...

The Science Behind Why Scams Work

＊ ＊ ＊ ＊ ＊ ＊ ＊ ＊ ＊ ＊

Even smart people fall for scams. Why do scams work? Scam artists see weaknesses. They assume people are greedy. Greedy people want more money. They want something for nothing. They want to get rich quick. They'll believe all kinds of things. Scam artists feed this greed. They fool people. They say there's a big prize. They also play off people's pride. They say nice things. They make people feel special. Some people are too trusting. Scam artists take people for granted. They trick them. They say they need help. People want to help. So they fall for the scam. Scam artists gain people's trust. Then people are less likely to ask questions. They don't see the truth. They believe the lies.

GLOSSARY

bigamy (BIH-guh-mee) the act of marrying someone while already married to another person

catfishing (CAT-fish-ing) the scam of tricking someone into a relationship by using a fake online profile or identity

confidence (KAHN-fuh-duhns) the feeling of belief or certainty

convicted (kuhn-VIK-tuhd) having been declared guilty of a criminal offense by a jury

defraud (dih-FROD) to obtain money from someone by deception

forger (FOR-juhr) a person who makes a copy or imitation for the purpose of deception

green goods scam (GREEN GUHDZ SKAHM) a scam that involves tricking people into buying counterfeit money made with stolen government plates

heiress (AYR-uhss) a woman who is legally entitled to the property or rank of another upon that person's death

mark (MAHRK) a target or victim of a scam

medium (MEE-dee-uhm) a person claiming to be in contact with the spirits of the dead and to talk between the dead and the living

pen pals (PEN PALZ) people who become friends by exchanging letters

pickpockets (PIK-pah-kuhts) people who steal from people's pockets

readings (REE-dings) using psychic powers to see a person's past, present, and future

scams (SKAHMZ) dishonest schemes or frauds

scam artists (SKAHM AR-tists) people who perform scams in order to get money

shill (SHIL) a person who helps a scam artist by acting as an enthusiastic customer

visions (VIH-zhuhns) vivid mental images, especially of the future

LEARN MORE!

Brown, Jordan D. *Fooled Ya!: How Your Brain Gets Tricked by Optical Illusions, Magicians, Hoaxes & More*. Lake Forest, CA: Moondance Press, 2017.

DuMont, Brianna. *Famous Phonies: Legends, Fakes, and Frauds Who Changed History*. New York, NY: Sky Pony, 2014.

DuMont, Brianna. *Thrilling Thieves: Liars, Cheats, and Cons Who Changed History*. New York, NY: Sky Pony, 2018.

INDEX